This Late Hour

This Late Hour

Poems by

Burt Myers

© 2023 Burt Myers. All rights reserved.
This material may not be reproduced in any form, published,
reprinted, recorded, performed, broadcast,
rewritten, or redistributed without
the explicit permission of Burt Myers.
All such actions are strictly prohibited by law.

Cover design by Burt Myers
Cover art by Matteo Catanese from Unsplash

ISBN: 978-1-63980-247-0

Kelsay Books
502 South 1040 East, A-119
American Fork, Utah 84003
Kelsaybooks.com

*To Andrée,
for always and everything*

Contents

I

Drought	13
A Dream of Leaving	14
Three Boys	15
Prodigal	16
Fall Landscape	17
Cowboys in Winter	18
The Bridal Party	19
The Puzzle	20
First Deer at Dawn	21
Reflection	22
Dressing in the Dark	23
My Other Self	24
For Every Stone	25

II

Opening Day	29
Exes	30
The Sunday Visits	31
Our Promises	32
The Magician's Assistant	33
Letters to a Married Man	34
The Yellow Scarf	35
Grain	37
Café Terrace at Night	38
Ghost	39
Silver Screen Queens	40
Settled	42
Sonnet after Shakespeare	44

III

Hollow	47
Threnody at Daybreak	48
Clouds Above the Nursing Home	49
Last Leaves	50
Sweet Pink Youth	51
At the Casino	52
Midnight Drive	53
Undressed	54
Taste	55
Nanna's Accordion	56
Grandpa's Garlic	57
March	59
Sisters	60

IV

Rosewood	63
No Telling	64
Acute	65
Red	66
Wordless	67
At the Gallery	68
A Walk at Otsiningo Park	69
Our House on Fire	70
Happy Home	71
Never a Handshake	72
The Soft Spiral	73
Say Love	75
Perennial	76

I

Drought

In this city of idiot grins, it's always raining.
A smattering of birds feather to confetti
over the shabby rowhouses straining
against the horizon. "Is it April already?"

asks my imagined companion. I'm shivering.
We walk together till the streets narrow,
ignoring the refuse in our path, piss rivering
the gutters, into some unfamiliar borough.

I try to meet her eye, blunder into a puddle
and fall. She unveils an umbrella. I take her
hand and lean into the gravity of her shadow.
She lifts me up, dry in a marigold slicker.

A Dream of Leaving

I didn't come home for the AM radio,
for the six months of filthy winter,
for the gone-to-dross department stores.

I came to see my sun rise in your sky
again, in the place I owned as home.
What's left is as much obligation as love.

Your drapes open to slate gray and silt,
to clouds an ever-present bruise.
I will not surrender to your weather.

Here there's only rain, only overcast,
nothing but water in all its forms—
a flood, and still you're dying of thirst.

I ache to be sun-seared and sky-blind,
defenseless in the face of something,
anything, someone. Let us face our own

horizons and their lights' diminishing:
One mother and one mother's son,
stir crazy and drunk for some ghost city.

What will I do with your one body
save watch it decay, wait for it to fail?
Wrap me in your arms one final time

before one or the other of us bolts down
some inevitable highway, leaving the soot
and sludge and the other one behind.

Three Boys

In every photo, we're lined up—
little, bigger, biggest—
three versions of the same boy

with the same bowl haircuts
and the same passed-along clothes,
like Russian nesting dolls.

Mom and Dad would take
the two of them, stack them up,
split me open and drop them

inside my ample lower half,
where I could keep them close.
I carry them like half-forgotten toys.

Dad has been lost and Mom
is in pieces. My brothers are safe
and unbroken inside me.

Prodigal

I want to write an elegy
for me, for all I might have done,
apologize to anyone
expecting bigger, braver things.
And I hear Etta James. She sings
it loud. As grievers pay respects,
her sly contralto resurrects
the prospects of the prodigy.

But Etta's part ends up recast,
and in her place some mock John Cage,
head bowed above a noteless page
and silent middle C, resists
the urge to play, his balled up fists
an ode to promise unfulfilled,
the block chords blocked, the fills distilled
to empty air. It's not at last

a satisfying epitaph,
but all that comes to meet my pen.
Some puffed-up rector rises then
for scripture, eulogy and psalms.
He hesitates, with upraised palms,
and waits for silence all around.
From way in back, the only sound—
one clever schoolboy's hectoring laugh.

Fall Landscape

A photographer showed up at my door,
dragged me outside, and said, "Look at this."
He pointed past my Japanese maples
to the sun dropping onto the horizon.

"Let me take some pictures," he said,
already clicking away, "and I'll make
a giant print, as big as your living room,
which I'll sell to you for a modest fee."

I'd never noticed this particular view
and agreed that I might like to see it again.
"Give me some time to save the money,"
I said, and sent him away. Week after week,

I'd cash my Friday paycheck and sneak
a single brick home from the yard.
I'd stash a twenty under a sofa cushion,
and cement that brick over the window.

By the following fall, I was ready—
$1,000 cash and fifty-two bricks
covering the window on the west wall.
One day the photographer returned.

I handed over the cash, showed him in,
and said, "Put it there." He did, and left.
I sat in the recliner, tipped it way back,
and fell asleep staring into the sun.

Cowboys in Winter

The Sons of Katie Elder make such noise!
Dad's fast asleep, despite his three grandsons
waving their toy pistols, kiddy cowboys
shouting to be heard above John Wayne's guns.

Mom sits out in the kitchen, where the din
is slightly less ear-splitting, with her boys.
We try to talk, but can't seem to begin;
glad for the kids and their disruptive toys.

The doctors say it's spreading quickly now.
And still it seems there must be some mistake.
Mom does what women do, fights through somehow
to give him what he needs when he's awake;

still throws the curtains wide each day at dawn
to what remains of winter's weakening sun.

The Bridal Party

The bridal party blocks the road
for pictures on the fieldstone bridge.
I slow the Mazda, watch their lavish
dance, the twill and taffeta twirl,

the clench of girls in turquoise gowns,
their boys in tuxes starched and stiff.
Now winding down, the hard part done,
they plume into the sun, and freeze,

the only movement morning's rain
from blazing silver maples, whose
drip rings entwine across the creek
behind the bride and prideful groom.

He looks up, sees me, points, and has
the party part to let me pass,
and on my driver's side one bridesmaid
smiles her lightest smile and waves,

and for an instant I'm the President,
as my slow-moving motorcade
wades gently through adoring crowds,
through princesses and paparazzi.

Then in my rear-view mirror they
turn back toward each other and
I watch those strapless backs and straight
black shoulders come together,

faces golden in the autumn sun,
ebullient at being here
to join this bride and groom, in just
this spot, on such an afternoon.

The Puzzle

Her interests dwindle
to a jigsaw puzzle
in a single lamp's circle.

I try to see her world's
narrowing as a sharpening
of focus. But I want her

to fight, to yell, to take
great fistfuls of pieces
and heave them against

the wall. Give me that
anger, and I will meet it
note for shivery note.

Instead, we talk calmly
over a newly unboxed puzzle,
picking out the straight-

edged pieces. She looks
for bits of ground and grass
and I for ice-blue sky.

Like this, we make our way
toward each other, working
slowly to square our ends.

First Deer at Dawn

Dad says the deer
rise well before the sun.
Our forest is silent,

the dark and cold
are hammer and brad.
He bears it stoically,

squirrels me at the bole
of a pine and trudges on
to the ridge above.

I shoulder the shotgun
to fuss at the gun gloves,
duck into the collar

of the blaze orange
hunting parka, and grouse
at the raw dawn. When a

buck wanders into view,
cold bones hedge the trigger;
an end to adolescence.

I quail, let him pass
and wait for my father.
The earth softens slowly.

Reflection

A well-pressed Donald Draper nurses a scotch,
framed by a swirling cloud of cigarette smoke.
He's haloed in amber light, his Brylcreemed hair
glistening beneath a smart fedora, crisp catchlights
in steely eyes, as he waits for this week's girl.

I'm on a bus to the city, *Mad Men* on my iPad.
Don is tastefully positioned screen right, looking
thoughtful against a warm bar-bronze background.
Suddenly, in the dark at his left, something moves
and my focus shifts to a ghostly face in the haze,

someone squatter, squarer, going gray, an old man
looking back at me: Me, an art director too,
but for a second-rate agency in a third-tier town,
a guy who could have really been something,
former up-and-comer on some slow road down.

Dressing in the Dark

It's wonderfully new,
this predawn ritual,
this purposeful silence
almost like prayer—

to dress with her there
in our darkened room,
gentle out a dresser drawer,
shuffle into underwear,

high-step into slacks,
thumb buttons up to holes,
drop the wingtips
to the hardwood floor,

then slip the silk up
snug to a crisp collar
and twirl it to two loops
folded over and knotted,

not quite perfect without
the light and mirror,
but all the more pleasing
for the imperfection.

Finally—she waits for it—
cupped coins and keys
released to a wool pocket,
a hand at the small

of her back, a kiss,
sometimes a bit more,
then footfalls fading, and
the door, carefully closed.

My Other Self

And that other self, who watches me from the distance of decades, what will she say?

—Jane Hirshfield

I know I've disappointed him again—
the man I'll one day be, or might have been.
There's no escape. One rheumy eye absorbs
my every move. The lazy second orb's
bemused by something scuttling up the wall.
The truth holes up. Somehow he sees it all.
He never rests, and never lets things go.
From out across the years, he'll let me know
when I've been stubborn, wrong, or stone asleep
as opportunity crept by. He'll keep
that eye peeled as I turn our other face
away. He follows, hauls his massive ass
to join me at the fridge night after night.
Together, we feed his boundless appetite.

For Every Stone

After Maggie Smith

For every stone thrown at a bird, there are
a million birds, and each with a song.
For every broken bone, there are a million
parents working to keep their children whole.
A mother thinks she can protect her child
from the half-horrific beauty of the world,
just as every barren woman seeks solace
in the calm of an empty afternoon. We sell
ourselves a bill of goods, claim comfort
in the giving up. We fixate on the dazzle
and call it up in flames. This world, this
wild, weird, beautiful place, this shithole—
if I had a daughter I'd share every bit of it,
every exquisite, detestable minute of it.
And when the wide-open world inside her
is littered with difficult questions with no
easy answers—watch me then, still singing.

II

Opening Day

Even on television, even
in drizzly upstate New York, four hours
from the dazzling new ballpark in Queens,
it's opening day. Our heroes trot
onto the diamond, joyful as teens
preening on some big-city sandlot,
and relax into their bright routines,
dancing, undefeated, through the showers,
with all of summer to believe in.

Exes

Without her there's only the dull hum
of morning, and the monitor's glare.
The words, when they finally come,
are nothing more than tired reflexes,
dumb glyphs blacking that white square.

A ladybug drops from the ceiling,
all the day's color on her quarter-inch back.
I long to blot out all I'm feeling,
and type a few-hundred Garamond X's,
then a screenful in Helvetica Black.

X's for kisses, for sex and subversion,
for censure, erasure, abstraction, consent.
I stand—hoping to find in diversion,
in the turn from our war of the sexes
and its unwritten apologies, some intent

beyond the holes punched in the page—
and carry the ladybug out to the lawn,
my psyche not ready today to engage
with the rest of the alphabet, the nexus
of our brief biography, with all that's gone.

The Sunday Visits

He has his girls each Sunday afternoon.
Their mother cracks the door and sighs "hello,"
then scowls. "You're drinking?" "No," he says, "hell no."
The girls are breaking up at some cartoon.

She goes to get them ready, makes him wait,
then leaves them to him with familiar kisses.
He pulls them close, immersed in all he misses.
"Just have them home by seven. Don't be late."

They'll see a movie down on Clinton Street,
the shabby second-run house by the pier.
He sneaks in dimestore candy, Cokes, a beer,
then sinks, between them, heavy in his seat.

Our Promises

Our promises were hard to make,
a second chance we had to take.
But what, at first, felt tentative,
became a way we might forgive
each other, for our daughter's sake.

You swallowed that familiar ache.
I tried, with so much still at stake.
But sometimes our desires outlive
our promises.

And so, mistake compounds mistake,
what once was clear becomes opaque,
and then there's no alternative
to quitting, nothing more to give,
and nothing left to do but break
our promises.

The Magician's Assistant

The conjurer lies lifeless in the tank,
the water going still, the cuffs secure—
another test of what he can endure,
or just another stunt, a stupid prank?

This wasn't in the ad! He's such a prick.
He's always testing me, the masochist—
a chainsaw at my waist, rope at my wrist.
The more depraved, the more he likes the trick.

Our audience is small tonight, and rough.
The tent is hot. They're bored and unimpressed.
He's at his worst, and even at his best
he's insecure. He's never good enough,

and takes it out on me, and on the act.
He wants to be Houdini, Penn or Teller,
but fears himself a fraud, some Uri Geller.
He stays on script on nights the place is packed,

but shows like this one there's no guarantee.
The crowd leans in and waits for the reveal.
The whispers start: "C'mon, this can't be real."
Well I, for one, ain't waitin' round to see.

I'll not be fodder for the fucking cops.
I swear he told me not to interfere,
and I don't need this shit. I'm out of here!
There always some new charmer needing props.

Letters to a Married Man

I steam it open like I always do,
hands shaking at the old pot-bellied stove,
then steel myself to face the thing, the love
her every line evades, and read it through.

The letters still show up from time to time,
less often these last years, but still they come,
each scented with her fusty vague perfume,
addressed, in that familiar hand, to him.

No mention anymore of what had been,
no plea to meet, no promises, no pledge,
no hope for his reply. No need to dredge
up all those arid arguments again.

He couldn't live two lives and so he chose.
He doesn't think I know. She's "just a friend"—
there's nothing to admit, nor to defend,
no reason to resent her chaste "hellos,"

her boasts of some sophisticated life,
the Taj Mahal, the Mediterranean cruise,
the preening travelogue that she calls news.
No mention of her husband, or this wife,

of grandkids, or of any life beyond
the fancy first-class flights. She closes with
the same thing every time, "Yours, Meredith."
He'll be home soon. I fold the cotton bond.

The glue stick's in his office top desk drawer.
I smooth the flap with one thin fingernail,
then tuck the envelope among the mail
stuffed in the box just outside our front door.

The Yellow Scarf

When he tells the story
of their long marriage
it always starts with this:
the yellow scarf—

the exact shade, he says,
of the mustard fields
around the shabby villa
they rented in Tuscany.

He found it in a shop
along the Arno,
a memento of the trip
and a birthday gift,

woven of the softest
lambswool. Today, as he
regales their young visitor
with the old story,

he fumbles a spoonful
of coffee, and she hands
him the scarf and he
takes it, not noticing,

wipes up the spill
and swabs his brow.
He stops then, looks down,
then around the room.

With a sheepish grin
and a wave of the hand,
his fist a flourish of gold,
he shrugs, hands it back

to his wife, grateful
these days for the simple
utility of things,
and returns to his story.

Grain

He found transcendence once, ages ago,
in the hard white glint of noonday sun
reflecting off a grain elevator on some endless
wheat field in the flat heart of Kansas,

the yellow crop bristling in the breeze,
the air in the shade cool and still, the horizon
stretching to forever in all four directions,
the railroad lines in and out ruler-true.

* * *

It carried him back to early summers
in the Pińczów railyard, where his steady gaze
met the unsayable, and the air was thick,
always, with the acrid smell of creosote,

where he measured the days by the angle
of the light, the depth of the shadows,
the precise amber of the grain beneath
the weighbridge, the shuttling of boxcars.

* * *

The past surrenders, now, with the sunset,
when the wide blemished sky of history,
of a heritage lost—grandparents, cousins,
great aunts and uncles gone—goes purple

and indistinct in shadow. It's all there, still,
in the soft tissue, a small knot going gold,
twisted and persistent, one with the sun
setting, getting smaller but never quite gone.

Café Terrace at Night

After the painting by Van Gogh

Down cobbled streets beneath a cobalt sky
we walk to dinner. On the café terrace
our table's glowing gold. The lantern light
illuminates both guests and passersby.
Tomorrow she'll be heading back to Paris,
and I Marseille. We've only got this night.

The couple at the table to our right
are arguing, and stop just long enough
to order two more pints of local beer.
And to our left, two lovers watch them fight.
He leans in close, says something, and they laugh.
And we laugh, too, just happy being here.

It's been so long. We live so far apart,
and never found a way to have each other.
Unsettled weeks turned into months, to years,
and now it's too late. Long past losing heart,
we've learned to cherish these scant hours together,
to prize a night like this when it appears.

Ghost

She was young once,
gawky and gamine
and just plain good.
Good, and all of seventeen,
before some ghost of a chance
handed her Hollywood,

before the machine turned
her into just another
extra-buxomed starlet
like every other,
lipsticked scarlet
and peroxided blonde.

Now, when casting calls
she's the damsel in distress,
the hard-ass redeemable sinner,
the winsome down-on-her-
leading-man mess,
or the high-style stunner who falls,

inexplicably,
for the dashing-in-dotage auteur
as delusional muse.
And it's her but it's not her—
her buoyance made bubbly,
her funk gone slow blues,

her savvy turned slickness,
intelligence to pluck,
quick spark to slow burn.
So many idiosyncrasies to unlearn,
all those new ways to undress,
and a life's work dismissed as dumb luck.

Silver Screen Queens

I love late-night TV, enthralled by old
time stars in black and white, those seminal
celebrities my grandma's age: the bold

sleek bob of Louise Brooks, her animal
desire constrained by just the halt and stammer
of scratchy silent-era cinema;

and Audrey Hepburn's sparkly, wide-eyed glamour—
that lilting accent and exquisite long
neck—the epitome of grace and grandeur;

then Rosemary Clooney, standing up to Bing
and singing brassy jazz or, years before,
Mitch Miller kitsch she hated all along;

and Doris Day, a sweetheart I adore,
another singer, whose *Pillow Talk* reveals
some spice behind the wholesome girl next door;

to Ginger Rogers, light but fierce, who steals
her scenes and dances every step with Fred
while, as she once said, backwards and in heels;

Shirley MacLaine too, the audacious redhead.
A sexy harlot, sure, but I like best
those times she played it innocent instead.

Yes, you might say I'm just a bit obsessed
with all these vintage heartthrobs, all their stirring
performances, the poise they each possessed.

What strange and silvery alchemy enduring
through the ages makes them still so appealing,
so fine, so outrageously alluring,

and so ignites this foolish fire I'm feeling—
besotted; set, by second reel, to reeling;
and wide awake now, staring at the ceiling?

Settled

My headstrong sixteen-year-old son
says, over takeout Vietnamese,
that he will never *settle* as,
he makes it clear, his dad has done.

So sure of everything! It makes
this father proud to know his boy
sees past the comfort they enjoy
to all his parents' worst mistakes.

You can't explain that's what life *is*—
the house outgrown, the job gone stale.
The marriage too. Sometimes we fail.
The awkward, brooding silences;

that we react, regret, regroup;
that raw ambition wilts with age;
that every Shakespeare turns the page
to fill the stage and feed his troupe.

Nor can you tell him how it feels
to see his mother's eyes in his,
how promise pales beside what is,
the twists that only time reveals.

I don't know where one might begin
to get at how a mind matures,
how eccentricity endures,
grows comfortable within its skin;

that though sometimes we still succumb
to jealousy, bad faith, wrong turns;
dumb luck and perseverance earns
the compromises we become.

I say "I know just how you feel.
Yes, chase your dreams and find good work."
I trade my chopsticks for a fork.
His carve the air with perfect zeal.

Sonnet after Shakespeare

Desiring this man's art and that man's scope,
desiring fame and fortune, each in turn,
I watch the masters scuffle and I learn
that art subsists on haughtiness and hope.

And scope? The young apprentice, for his part,
allows desire to spark, then lets it burn
to incandescence no one love could earn,
and turns the dying embers into art.

A journeyman, like me, who learns to cope
with fate and failure, not so strong or smart,
who buries his desire deep in his heart,
whose art too often tends to shopworn trope,

remembers how the drive to art inspires,
loves, more than what he makes, what he desires.

III

Hollow

She watches a thin rain
fall, grim and meager,
saturating the playground

across the grit-gray two-lane,
where some little leaguer
slops onto the mound.

As she waits out a migraine
with radio-staticky Grieg, her
neighbor's lank bloodhound

heaves at a thick chain,
defending his beleaguered
patch of muddy ground.

Crows veil the wind vane.
The long days fatigue her.
On the ballfield, kids pound

their mitts and yell, complain-
ing to no one, just eager
to hear that hollow sound.

Threnody at Daybreak

The hoarfrost trims the fence posts.
She muses at the window, watches while
the chipmunks maze the woodpile
as black tea steeps and pumpernickel toasts.

She sets her place, quells a yawn,
still focused on a backyard lost in shade,
then uncaps the marmalade.
Red finches jounce the feeders, seed the lawn;

the oaks surrender dry leaves.
Soon she's done, save a final wedge of bread.
The rake is in the boatshed,
she thinks. But where are his gardening gloves?

She washes her few dishes
as sunlight climbs across the gabled roof,
then, the kitchen clean enough,
tromps to the mudroom for his galoshes.

Clouds Above the Nursing Home

Remember clouds? Remember having time
for clouds? Remember how we thought we'd climb
the backyard elm to get a better view?
And thinking that was all we had to do?

For eighty years I walked this crumbling town,
its broken pavement, always looking down
in search of someone else's mislaid change.
I forgot the sky, how it would rearrange

itself as we lay spellbound on the grass,
collecting shapes as they would slowly pass,
or as they'd swiftly metamorphosize,
from clown to car to kids before our eyes.

The nurses won't allow us on the grounds,
and everything reminds me now: the mounds
of bleach-burned pillows, pill-jar cotton balls,
Jane's gauzy perm careering down the halls.

These days, the only clouds I see are carved
from pasty film school dropouts' summer-starved
obsessions. All the shapes are theirs, not mine,
and shrunk to fit some smaller storyline.

Last Leaves

Autumn's last leaves fill
the rusty red wagon
our children abandoned
(they grew up and left),
three-wheeled and forgotten,
a sad hobbled planter
for Annie, to spice
up the backyard, I guess.

Our winters are tranquil
now, no brash toboggans,
no pucks on the pond
and no forts in the drifts,
no handmade knit mittens
dispatched to Atlanta,
to pack snow to ice
in our grandchildren's fists.

No, they never had kids, all
our sons, fine young men.
Come Christmas they'll send
up their big-city gifts,
and none of us, not one,
will bother with Santa
(or think about Christ),
or pretend, anymore, he exists.

Sweet Pink Youth

You always say one day you'll get in shape,
lose the weight, start running again,
you and the dog up at six and out in the sun,
loping among the pines out back,
circling the high school's cinder track,

and then there's a spot or a lump or a cold
that won't go away, and the phone call comes,
and you're winded like you've never been,
that punch-in-the-stomach bad news leaving
you slumped in your front hall, chest heaving,

promising to God, to anyone and everyone,
a new man, a better life, a thousand good
deeds done for some miracle medical advance,
for one more chance at fitness, at health,
at exuberant, immortal, sweet pink youth,

at anything but death and her grim nonchalance,
her mocking dance with the truth.

At the Casino

As horsemen move from long to longer shots
and poker sharps to rash, then reckless, bets,
four ladies feed crisp twenties to the slots,
the air around them stale with cigarettes.

They while away a summer afternoon.
Free margaritas loosen up the purse.
The house will have their cut, and all too soon
a run of luck dissolves to bad, then worse.

They break for dinner, one ahead, three not,
and talk turns to oncologists and kids.
They're, each of them, at war with the disease.
Then *back to the machines!* They laugh a lot,
lay down their hard-won cash despite the odds,
and celebrate unlikely victories.

Midnight Drive

You looked up to me blankly,
old gray herringbone flat cap
soft in your hands. I just stared,

long-drive worn and hard-news jarred,
not sure what to say. The nurse
beside you broke our silence

with the simple, grim details:
your race to the hospital
in the middle of the night,

Mom unconscious on the way,
stable but comatose now;
the hours you waited alone.

You were lost, we all were, those
next days, waiting for the end.
We've never talked about it,

whether it still troubles you,
still keeps you awake at night,
five years on, at ninety-four;

nor of how you made that drive
in the blurred cataract light.
I wonder if it haunts you

still, as it does me—that night,
those milk blue hands, your face turned
up as if to ask, "What now?"

Undressed

My mother's tissue-paper skin hangs loose
and plum gray at the IV, and across
the multiple incisions at her breast,
her neck, her abdomen. She's been undressed,

her secrets bared through folds of flimsy gown
as, gingerly, the nurses help her down
to bed and struggle on her underwear.
She runs a bone-cold hand through thinning hair.

I think about the months to come, if we
have months; the layman's blade that peels away
our stale propriety like onionskin
to leave us stripped to myth, astonished in

the face of all the things we've never said,
the awkward hours and brutish days ahead,
the pride that must be, finally, forsaken,
the cancer rampant now, her body broken.

Taste

Grief wells up from the earth,
metallic, black and acrid,
salt sour and pooling, sacred
and heavy in her mouth.

Two attendants deliver
a spray of roses. She lays them out
across his worsted wool suit,
as old friends palaver,

each mirroring the next's
wistful pinguid stance
in some flat-footed dance
they imagine resurrects

an era gone. They telescope
the restive, formal tension
in some elemental misapprehension
to hope beyond hope.

She turns away and swallows hard.
The thin skin of bonhomie
is stripped to awkward reverie
in the hearse to the graveyard,

the first of many dissembled days,
her life now lost to epilogue,
appetite to bilious fog,
truth to facile, fatuous praise.

Nanna's Accordion

Nanna's accordion
is gathering dust
on a plywood floor
at the top of the stairs.

She got it in '41,
back when she was just
a child, before the war.
Kids themselves, her heirs

can't bear its squawking spirit,
its raw asthmatic
rasp, or its wheezing
sick-room breath.

They imagine they hear it,
even from the attic;
a sound once pleasing,
now too much like death.

Grandpa's Garlic

Grandpa's garlic still grows wild,
the tender buds as white as milk.
Subsumed by spurge and jimsonweed,
his long-abandoned gardens choke,

the backyard giving way to wood,
the chicken wire to rust, the oak
posts rotting in the ground he'd wedged
apart with his old railroad pick.

When I was just a child, he'd wield
the hoe and shovel, me the rake,
until that ordered square we walked
was blossoming with honest work.

* * *

Most days we'd hike the hollow, wend
among the pines and tamarack,
the old, deserted mines, the wide
stone trail. With pocketknives, we'd hack

the anthracite that laced the shale, would
haul our pails through trash and rock
—the hillside scarred, an open wound—
then round to home. The sturdy brick

house beckoned; Nanna's kitchen warmed
for dinner. I would help her cook,
then slip away while Grandpa washed
the dishes, back to that day's book.

* * *

I fell to sleep, and fell, fast-forward
through the years, to here—a shock
of gray, bad back, days overworked
and underpaid, long nights awake—

to this insomniac dawn, a world
removed, three decades on, to pack
his last possessions. Pointed toward
the long ride home, the rental truck

squats in the yard. A brittle wind
numbs our procession—shunt and stack,
his boxed belongings heaped like cordwood,
just tomorrow's yard sale junk.

* * *

And so his garden's gone to weed—
to seed, they say—and any talk
of changing that is only talk, we'd
sooner turn the old man's clock

around, unbend his spine, unwind
the years, and send him spinning back
to fruitful youth. But while the wood
takes back the lawn, each pallid stalk

lives on, and fumbles heavenward
and greens. And yet unseen, his garlic,
pungent prize, marble-hard reward,
plumbs the rich earth, the soil's coal black.

March

One Saturday, the second week in March,
our valley sees high-pressure fronts collide
and suddenly it's sixty-eight degrees
and fine as Independence Day outside.

House finches flower the backyard maple trees,
announcing spring. Across the neighborhood
a foot of snow dissolves in half a day,
the last few silty mounds becoming mud.

It's quiet now. The Whitehursts are away,
and from my porch I look out on their yard
littered with last fall's toys, Amanda's muck-
moored dump truck buried to its yellow hood.

My father worked construction, drove a truck
like that, its tires as tall as me. He spent
the summers building highways, winding through
our state's small towns, wherever the jobs went.

He was born in March and died in March too.
Hard to believe he's nearly eight years gone—
gone longer than Amanda's been alive.
It's quiet now. But time bulldozes on,

and soon enough, I know, spring will arrive,
for real this time. The Whitehursts will return,
the midday sun will reach this narrow porch,
our close-cropped yards will desiccate and burn.

Sisters

The sisters, quick
to gather,
like moths to candlewick,
mourn another
sudden death,
with thrumming
talk and measured breath.
Their men succumbing
one by one,
they rally round
the common family good
and carry on,
stoic and sorrowbound,
in widowhood.

IV

Rosewood

She plays, my virtuoso troubadour.
Her slender fingers never seem to rest.
And I, just like her cherished old guitar,
come thrumming at her light and sure caress.

She vamps along the cutaway of collarbone,
her drumming heart thumping time with mine,
and sings a gentle "yes" into the hollow,
her fingers spidered down my fretboard spine,

then slings a practiced arm across my waist,
my bout of belly, strumming out our sound,
and I moan low and large, her doghouse bass,
as rich as rosewood, resonant and round.

Our bold crescendo meets a rousing hand.
I shout, "Bravo! Encore!" I love this band.

No Telling

While Mississippi John Hurt fingerpicks
his "make me down a pallet on your floor,"
Jack lies in bed, anticipating sex.
Jan storms in, throws her ring down, slams the door,

not to go out, but just to raise the stakes.
The record skips—"Don't let my good girl catch . . ."
then, *scriiitch*, "might cut and starve you too." It takes
a moment for Jack's heart, and Hurt, to snatch

back that familiar twelve-bar melody
and to reclaim its steady alternating bass.
Jan doesn't say a word, won't meet his eye,
just waits for him to make his sorry case.

"I'm not . . ., it won't . . .," he stammers, "You are such
a spiteful bitch. Why can't you let it rest?"
"She wasn't . . ., I don't . . ." Now he's said too much,
confirming things that Jan had only guessed.

She grabs the record, breaks it in her fist.
He's gone too far. It's over now, she knows.
And Mississippi John? Well, he'll be missed.
But Jack? No telling where that trouble goes.

Acute

Vacancy's pulsing V trains its nadir
hard on the setting sun's alizarin
arpeggio. Inside, the neon's thin
staccato glow bleeds across my austere

room, where Thelonious Monk spins thick fists
of piano, angular and graceless, bop-hard,
as Rollins' tenor stabs, a jagged shard
in *Brilliant Corners*. What discordant twists

provoked my wanderlust—dazed ricochet
into this blank slate noir neighborhood,
blowing solo, sorrowful mad flood
miasmal blues gone muse-sick cabaret,

beating, off time, to Roach's brisk high-hat,
eyes on the deadbolt, knees tight to my chest?
The day is too far gone for getting dressed.
Monk, and *Well You Needn't,* squares with that.

Red

She's a bare ruby bulb,
a photojournalist's darkroom,
a fetishist's flash fire,
a blogger's dank bedroom.
She's a hair-trigger tripwire,
a backstreet bordello,
she's black cherry Jell-o
juiced up with Red Bull.

She's a warning flare, a stop sign,
my cardinal heart exposed,
a good Merlot on Friday night,
a single scrapbooked rose.
She's the muted crimson half-light
of a Brooklyn brownstone dawn.
She's a long, low siren song
bleeding across the phone line.

She's a brick smashing plate glass,
a Bic slashing manuscripts,
a Coney Island hot dog stall
and sticky candied-apple lips.
She's a sunburst Les Paul
through a vintage Fender Twin.
She's a bashful half grin
before a flushed first kiss.

She's a front porch full of fireflies,
the backyard dogwoods turning,
an ace of hearts tucked up a sleeve,
a kid's first Christmas morning.
She's fireworks on New Year's Eve
whose scarlet blossoms fill the air,
fresh fire and color everywhere,
jewels lighting my inviolate skies.

Wordless

Sometimes the diction
of emoticons is enough.
I can picture her smile
in the "lol," and offer fluff
in kind, all the while
imagining some fiction

in which we finally kiss
the keyboards goodbye
to meet in the raw world
for a stroll, and where I
gently take her hand,
or risk an arm across

her perfect, slender hips.
She'll meet my bashful gaze
and laugh for real, then
turn toward me, raise
her face to mine, and lean
to meet my wordless lips.

At the Gallery

There she is again! We're off
the bus. The crowd between us swells,
a scattered blur of snapshot smiles
soon swallowed by the gallery doors.

The ben-day blazoned lobby soars;
impassive abstracts line one wall—
Kandinsky, Rothko, Motherwell.
Not her, though. I'm not quick enough.

I'm waylaid by excited friends,
and caught up in the colloquy
with colleagues who know more than me,
know every artist, date and name.

I roam the aisles and bide my time.
She's two rooms down, now just ahead,
then lost across the colonnade.
At last, just as our visit ends,

at one end of the gallery,
where monolithic oils give way
to softer light and scumbled gray,
I study one fine miniature.

She rounds into my corridor,
stops short, turns shyly toward the piece.
There, side by side, we lean in close,
delighting in the delicacy.

A Walk at Otsiningo Park

April enters with a lark,
with one more after-season snow.
This walk, is this our new beginning—
figure-eights around the park,
the ballfields white for one more inning?
Winter's forever letting go.

The poet has our couple slow
one stanza in. See the way
he subtly moves outside the scene
to high among the trees? We know
he's looking for some hint of green.
Up there the white ground falls away.

He carries on, and up, so high
that all those leafless trees go dark.
The pond's a single frozen teardrop
mirroring a crisp blue sky;
the walkway, when our lovers stop
and kiss, is an infinity mark.

Our House on Fire

Nothing but this, then,
at the end of the day:
we watch the sky go gray
and the house go dense
with the same hard reticence
each evening ushers in.

Our failed manuscripts
catch fire, go up in flames.
The prolix book of names
curls into smoke, all those
epithets escaping to cellulose
before they pass our lips.

Everything disappears—
the office chair, the laptop,
the ugly torchière lamp
(a gift from her mother),
respect for one another,
the sex, the good years.

We watch until the last
of the cinders dull from red
to dust, then slump to bed
and char-hard dreams,
nothing quite as it seems
any more in our blackened past.

Happy Home

Back home again. Mom leaves on the light,
and when I've had a snootful, hers remains
the place I end a fruitless too-late night
with a fumbled housekey. She never complains,
just lets me in, and lets me feed my appetite

for loud debate. She puts the kettle on,
then lights two Luckys, passing one to me,
and hears me out. When I stumble to the john,
she hides her purse, puts up the cutlery,
sits patiently and waits. I'll soon be gone.

Never a Handshake

Buried under the hood of some
old Dodge Ram, he sees me pull in,
tucks away his wrench, slips around

the wide truck and across the bay,
toweling blackened hands, and greets
me just outside the garage door.

Never a handshake anymore,
since Dad passed; always a long hug,
his shirt oily and mine crisp white,

pressed tight. "It's the starter, I think."
He smiles, says he's good, pops the hood,
glad to help, sets the paying work

aside. He never takes a cent.
We lean close, gentle together,
staggered by middle age—fifty

unfathomable and on the
horizon—and talk as he works,
more distant, yet close as ever.

The Soft Spiral

I loved the soft spiral,
the worn pigskin floating
just over one pair of outstretched
hands and into the next, then
tight to my best friend's chest,

plays drawn up on dirty palms
in the language of some archaic
middle school library playbook—
flanker, fly, buttonhook—
or "just go out and get open."

We all loved those apple crisp
October afternoons, backyard
pickup games with fence posts for
goalposts, the spent garden out
of bounds, tackles soft on fallen

leaves, the tangled limbs
of sprawling boys who smelled
of grass and dirt and sweat,
of freshly laundered fleece.
Our sisters were forbidden then,

and later on distractions, thrust
into our midst by hormonal insistence,
by thirteen's confusion, then
fourteen's compulsion, to fistfights,
fat lips, and friendships disrupted.

We followed the seasons, blind
instinct impelled us, from
football to basketball, baseball
and back, whatever the weather,
this loose group of friends;

and even today, when we wind up
together, some dim recollection
brings back the emotion;
and the good guys back then,
the ones who played fair, who laughed

when they lost, stood up for
their friends, under the thickening
frames and the thinning gray hair
they're the same decent men
we trusted as boys, back then.

Say Love

The streams run with sweetness, fattening fish
—John Ashbery

Say love is hurtling toward you just this minute,
the instant that you turn and acquiesce
and, leaning into winter's barrenness,
shrug off the hope that you've invested in it.

Then say love finds you—say it's not too late,
despite your doubt—and offers what you covet.
Will you refuse? Will you make nothing of it?
When crocuses are blossoming, when great

blue heron glide upstream in ponderous flight,
feeding on mackerel and pompano
and darkening the river as they go,
will you keep to the shallows, out of sight?

Let's say that it's enough that love attends
to the black undertow you drag along,
your mixed feelings hesitant sparrow song
presaging spring. In time each season ends.

So let's say love appears to grant your wish—
that and spring rain. Embrace it. Reach for love
and for the chance to fly, just once, above
the thawing river and the fattening fish.

Perennial

She cooks a roast on Saturday.
After a gentle midday shower
that glossed the ground and cleared the air
and chased her children to their rooms,

we coax them back outdoors to play
in the yard. Her tulips are in flower.
We sit beneath a backyard pear
suddenly popcorned white with blooms.

She asks me, "Would you like to stay
the night?" and smiles. I ponder our
imagined future, how much I care
for her, and all my "yes" presumes.

And so, today, at this late hour,
we start. Elsewhere, the rain resumes.

Acknowledgments

Thank you to the editors of the journals in which the following poems first appeared, sometimes in slightly different form:

Angle Poetry: "Hollow," "Perennial," "Sonnet after Shakespeare"
Barrow Street: "A Dream of Leaving," "For Every Stone"
Birmingham Poetry Review: "Our House on Fire"
First Things: "Cowboys in Winter," "Nanna's Accordion," "Sisters"
The Hopkins Review: "Dressing in the Dark," "First Deer at Dawn"
Measure: "Drought," "Grandpa's Garlic," "Happy Home," "Letters from a Married Man" (as "The Letters"), "The Magician's Assistant," "March," "Never A Handshake," "Undressed"
Poetry East: "Reflection"
The Raintown Review: "Café Terrace at Night," "Last Leaves" (as "Autumn Lament"), "A Midnight Drive," "Red," "Settled," "Silver Screen Queens," "Wordless" (as ":-)")
The Rotary Dial: "The Sunday Visits," "Threnody at Daybreak"
The Shit Creek Review: "Rosewood"
The Southern Review: "Fall Landscape"
Stone Canoe: "Yellow Scarf," "Grain"
Tar River Poetry: "The Bridal Party," "Prodigal," "Sweet Pink Youth"
Think: "Acute," "At the Casino," "Opening Day," "Our Promises," "Say Love," "Taste"

"The Puzzle" was selected by Dana Gioia as winner of the NY Encounter 2020 Poetry Contest and published at: www.newyorkencounter.org/2020-poetry-contest.

Thank you to all the wonderful writers and organizers I've met at the many conferences I've attended, particularly those at Poetry by the Sea, the Sewanee Writers Conference, and the West Chester Poetry Conference. Special thanks to my workshop leaders Mark Jarman, David Mason, A.E. Stallings, Greg Williamson, and David Yezzi.

Thank you to Tara Betts, Mark Jarman, and David Yezzi for their generous words as I prepared this book for publication, and to Maggie Smith for her insightful and kind comments on the manuscript-in-progress.

A special thank you to my local writing group, the "Grapevine poets"—dear friends who keep me engaged, excited, and (on occasion) writing: Sharon Ball, Richard Braco, Joanne Corey, Merrill Douglas, Jessica Dubey, Myron Ernst, Carol Mikoda, Andrée Myers, Wendy Stewart, Susan Thornton, and J. Barrett Wolf.

Thank you to my family for their love and support (and for providing so much in the way of inspiration for the poems).

And thank you, above all, to my dear wife Andrée, who, in addition to being my first and best reader, provides me with all the love and support that any writer could ever hope for. Plus, she gets me out of the house and into the wild world, where the new poems are waiting to be discovered.

About the Author

Burt Myers's poems have been published in a number of notable journals, including *Barrow Street, The Hopkins Review,* and *The Southern Review.* A lifelong resident of upstate New York, he works as an art director at Binghamton University. He is also a singer-songwriter and guitarist, and his album *Love and the Lack Thereof* can be found on most common streaming services. He lives just outside of Binghamton with his wife, Andrée, and their dog, Bella.

www.ingramcontent.com/pod-product-compliance
Lightning Source LLC
Chambersburg PA
CBHW050846160426
43193CB00034B/2021